Free to be Me

Jo Hope

BookLeaf Publishing
India | USA | UK

Presentation by *BookLeaf Publishing*

Web: www.bookleafpub.com

E-mail: info@bookleafpub.com

ISBN:9789358314458

First edition 2024

DEDICATION

Grandma Olive and Uncle Chris.

"For those who understand, no explanation is needed. For those who don't, no explanation is possible."

ACKNOWLEDGEMENT

For my Son, without whom I quite simply wouldn't be here. O, I love you with every ounce of my being.

To my closest people, who keep my world turning, Cookey, Cooley, EClair, Flowers, PJ and RB; you always encouraged me at every step of being 'Free to be Me'.

Cookey, even though you are the furthest away, on the other side of the world; you're one of the 'lifers'. You've known me for thirty six years, little wonder we're both white haired, your beard is way more impressive though! I appreciate you more than I could ever say. You're my mainstay, you've always dragged me out of my dark times metaphorically by my hair and you never, ever give up on me. Here's to thirty six more!

Cooley, my High School curly-haired twin, where do I begin? You're the feisty to my calm, the zen to my tangent-fuelled mind and my fellow 'burning the midnight oil' creative. We embrace the sublime silence when the rest of the world is asleep. To re-quote your Andy Warhol quote; "It's a brand new, same old you." I remind myself of that, every day.

Eclair, my soul sister, and my dear friend. We have only been in each other's lives for a few years, but time knows no bounds when two souls meet and share as one. You've embraced me, flaws and all, and never left my side. Thank you, for always being there.

My Flowers, some eight years ago, after not seeing each other for over thirty years, I found you again. To say that that gap in time had made no difference whatsoever, is a huge understatement. You've been by my side during some very horrid and awful moments; but you've celebrated my biggest and best ones too. Thank you, for always being there.

PJ, yep!—despite the look on your face, I'm still 'talking' and you're still reading! Thank you, just for being you. I'm not sure you'll ever realise how instrumental you have been in so many of the words I've written here. Thank you, for the endless phone calls and PJ wisdom. Not sure where I would be without you—talking to myself probably…What did you say a while ago? "You're not broken, just bent!" Happen you were 'Wright'.

RB, even though we don't see each other, or speak as much nowadays—cause you're rubbish at communication! If anyone, over the years, has taught me about resilience; it's you. You'll always be a part of my story, we don't need to talk every six months to have a solid friendship, right? I am so proud of who you are, and everything you have achieved, thank you, for being you. In the words of Blink 182: I Miss You.

To my Mother, who would always say, "I don't know how you do it." I'm still not sure how I have either, but I have.

To my Dad, who heart-breakingly didn't live to see that I did do it. I know he would have told everyone that would listen, that I did.

Lastly, to my Riley, who knows exactly what he brings to my world. You always restore my faith, my hope and my belief in myself; to never stop doing what you say I do best. For all the patience you have had when I've proudly shown you a piece I've written sitting on the loo, (it's true) and for all your many hours of reading everything I've written, with as much enthusiasm as I've written it with. "Never opened myself this way, life is ours we live it our way. All these words I don't just say, and nothing else matters."

There have been many, many others who have supported me through the last 13 years, particularly. My dear Uncle Chris, Uncle Fred, Auntie Helen, it goes without saying, that you've always been there. Dorothy, Hels, Nat, Nick, Tasha, thank you for being on the other end of the phone in the small hours, every time one of you has helped me to see my way; you've had a huge part to play.

Hx

PREFACE

"I had to fall
To lose it all
But in the end
It doesn't even matter."
:Bennington, Bourdon, Delson, Hahn, Shinoda

Love is:

Love is patient,
Love is kind—

a place where no one is left behind,
the flaws we are but too blind to see,
the rose-coloured haze that envelops; capturing
perfectly

Love does not envy,
It does not boast—

embraces all things,
the gentle nurturing of laughter and the sad,
expresses gratitude for the blessings not
dwelling on the 'must haves'

Love is not proud,
It is not rude—

fosters an air of graciousness
where there is no attitude or pride
to be found,
no matter the moment, nor who is around

Love is not self-seeking,
It is not easily angered—

shows meekness, a sense of control;
soft voices which tread with care and humility
for the sake of all souls

Love keeps no record of wrongs,

counted misdemeanours,
favours no one

Love does not delight in evil,
It rejoices, with the truth—

goodness, spread by hands from our joy-filled
pockets of harmony, tenderness and integral
roots

always protects,

always trusts,

always hopes,

always perseveres,

Love never fails…

Based on: 1 Corinthians 13:4-8 (NIV)

You Have a Past

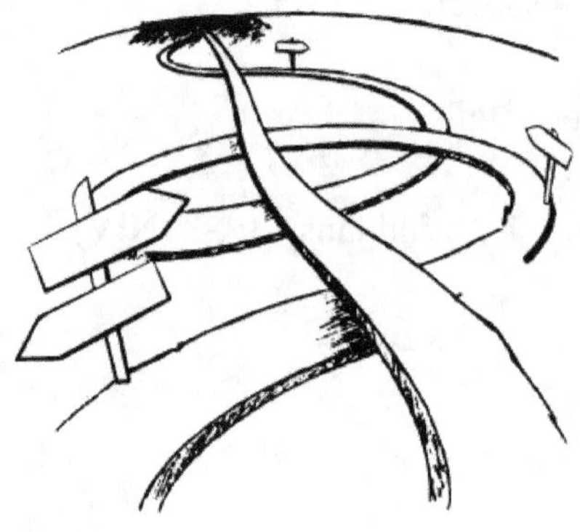

You have a past
I have a past

Acknowledge it
Accept it

Work on it
Accept it again

Eyes forward
Face front

Don't look back
You're not going that way.

Maybe a little glance over your shoulder every
now and then

That's okay
It's still there

But
It
Doesn't
Have
To
Control
You
Anymore

Eyes forward
Face front,
Don't look back,
You're not going that way…

Sometimes In Life

Sometimes, in life
life does not always pan out how you'd planned
hoped
or even wished for.

Sometimes, in life
life is rubbish
disappointing
you may feel let down
you may feel disheartened
ruined.

Sometimes, in life
life is simply just not how you wished it would
be but
sometimes, in life

you have to pick yourself up

drag yourself up
force yourself up
brush yourself off
and make yourself move forward.

You have to make yourself
regain the control
regain your dignity
regain your sanity even
and just keep on moving forward.

Sometimes, in life
you have to reflect, rethink, replan, and start
again

Sometimes, in life
you must make the most of the life you have
been blessed with
realise that life is factually too short
to be anything less than happy.

Wherever you are today
know that you are not alone,
know that you are special to someone
know that you are loved by someone
and that someone
may not be the someone you realise is there for
you right now
but they will be.

Life is,
for living
for loving
and giving

Life is,
for taking ownership of and
for accepting that it's not always rosy
but it's your life,
and you are in control of your own destiny.

Life is, yours
Life is, life.
It's down to you—no one else—to find your
place, your place in this world.

Would You Understand?

Would you understand,
if I said that I had dropped out of my soul?

Would you understand,
if I said I don't want to be this way, in this mind,
in this cage that traps me—yet I'm not a wing
clipped bird?

Would you retreat,
if I said that my mind is too messy,
that there's many boxes without lids,
so many undone,
so many left to stare at,
muddle through,
too many that need sorting out.
I need order,
I need lists,

I need space in my head but not for the things
that don't exist.

The past comes to haunt and smudges the lines
between then and now.
The past comes to haunt when I'm trying not to
think but somehow
it breaks through to my consciousness and taps
away at me,
picks at me,
irritates me,
shouts at me, until I run, with my eyes closed,
and I run until I can no longer hear.

Running gives me so much to aim for,
so much to look forward to,
so much to focus on and focus is what is
required.
Focus achieves, bad memories from the past do
too
but not when I don't want to...
not, when I don't want to relive,
realise,
reflect—I don't want to reflect,
I don't want to look in that mirror anymore.

So, I'll just wait,
I'll wait for that sweet voice that whispers... that
voice that beckons me into the light... that voice

that doesn't shout of the vitriolic past until I can
hear no more.
The voice that I love,
is the voice that I like to hear,
the soft, sweet voice of the future—the future
that remains so bright it blinds and deafens me
all at the same time.
The voice that welcomes me like the open arms
that welcome me
and the hand on my shoulder which calms me,
makes me patiently wait and makes me realise
that I am still here,
I'm still me,
I'm still locked into that cage but I have the
power to release myself;
for the lock was on the inside all along.

So, tomorrow, I will fly,
I will soar and I will-for now-imagine the air on
my face,
I will imagine the sounds,
the smells,
the sensory awareness that consumes me as I
look down upon all that has tried to keep me
down,
and keep me contained.

Tomorrow, I will be free…

Dear Younger Me

While you sit
hugging your tear soaked knees
the silence wrapped around your shoulders
every sound muffled
except the continuous, innocuous beating of
your heart
you can feel it in your chest
your throat
your ears.

You can taste it... I'm here for you.

While you look in the mirror
judging your reflection
your eyes focusing on the face looking back
every feature out of place
except that doesn't surprise you because
you hate all of your face

your eyes
your nose.

You can say it… I'm here for you.

While you walk to school
purposefully dawdling
your mind running in the opposite direction
every day wanting to stray
although it's little wonder when
the friends never stayed
not the good
not the bad.

You can feel it… I'm here for you.

While you try to wind down
drained and exhausted
your eyes fixed on everything in the dark
every night wanting to disappear
to slip away from reality
the dark hours linger
you want to be free
you want to be me.

You can heal it… I'm here for you.

'NO'

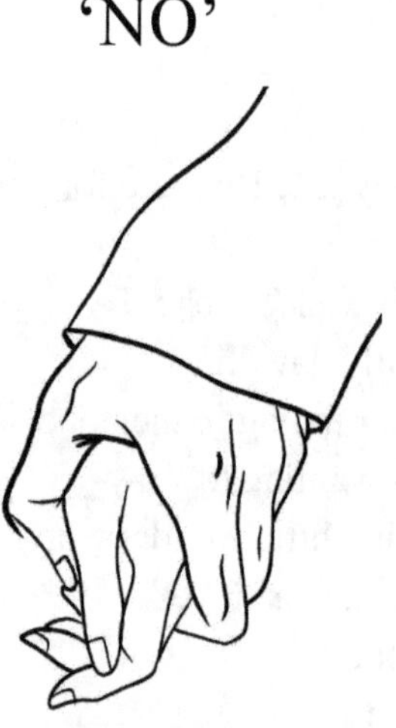

'NO' was a word you didn't understand
when you took me by the hand

from the bar
to your car
for another jar
in that bar
it wasn't far

you took me to land
waste land
dark land
wouldn't go there on your own in the dark land
only fit for waste land,

was I a waste?

as you pawed at my waist?
the haste…
the waste…

I was waste
my need to wait
was a waste
my chaste
was a waste
you made me feel like a waste
as you pawed at my waist
in the car
after the bar

when you took me by the hand,
'NO' was a word you didn't understand.

An Indelible Mark

An indelible mark
hard line
deep trace.

Can't be erased.

No matter the pace
the distance
the time.

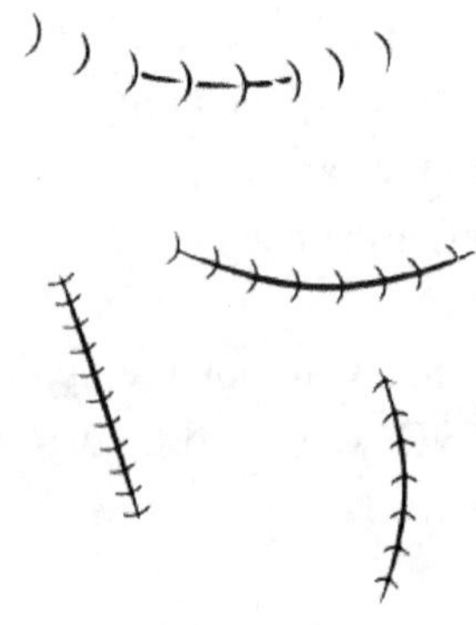

It lingers.

Like a nightmare
entwined
in my mind.

Can't be erased.

No matter the state
of my mind
any time.

Free to be Me

Someone once asked me what I wanted,
I answered 'to be free.'

Free to be me,
free to feel,
free to clothe my skin,
free to do what I wanted,
free to speak,
free to feel safe in my space,
free to express,
free to disagree,
free to laugh,
free to cry,
free to be me.

Free without threats,
violence,
restrictions,
fear…
imprisonment,
judgement,
verbal abuse,
my voice didn't matter,
no one would believe me;
I always lived in fear.

I still live in fear,
the fear that resides in my head.
I can't count the times I would wish I was dead.

I'd will him to kill me, to free me from pain;
but for me to die would only be his gain.

So I'd stay,
take the hits,
the punishment for being this way,

So I'd stay,
I'd promise myself I'd find the strength to leave
one day.

So I'd stay,
slowly erase myself,
surely everyone lived this way.

Someone once asked me what I wanted,
I answered 'to be free'.

Free to be me,
free to feel,
free to clothe my skin,
free to do what I wanted,
free to speak,
free to feel safe in my space,
free to express,

free to disagree,
free to laugh,
free to cry,
free to be me.

Now I am free.
Free to be me…

Panic!

It is possible
and that's not to say
there won't be moments, hours or days when
those old survival tactics creep;
but no longer control you,
taking you deep
and deeper still
into a world where to heal means
'take a pill'.

I often think I'm smashing life,
just generally doing okay
until a moment like this morning—
when a horrid start to the day—
woke me in the dark
I was hot
needed air
in a screaming, horrific panic
it made me feel the fear,

It's panic [I know I'm safe]
It's panic [I know I'm safe]

I know it's panic [why aren't I safe?]
I know it's panic [why aren't I safe?]
I flee my room
a brighter space
so many thoughts I have to erase
my heart in my throat, I'm going to choke
on my hidden years
running free like the tears
on my face
I can't pace
the crying
feels like dying

I no longer hold onto my tears
not like I used to
not like I had to
I'd cry into pillows
the crook of my arm; anything not to be heard
I'd hear myself trying to soothe, and hang on to
every last word
that I'd repeat in my head—
hide the dread
of fearing going to sleep
in the safety of my own bed.

My Pain

Migraine
Lives in my brain
Drives me insane
In my brain
The pain

It drains

and it drains

and drains

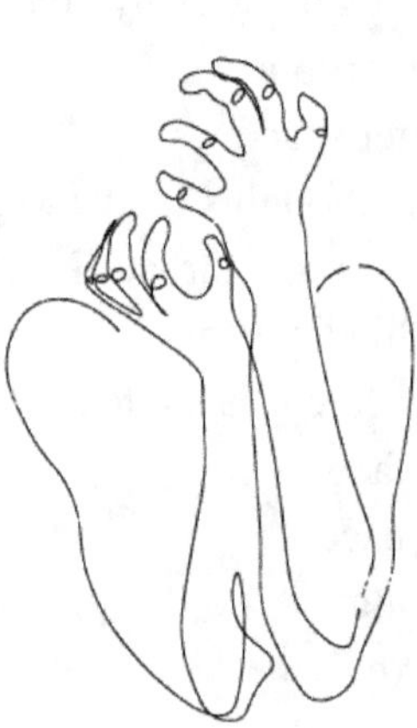

All the pain
In my brain
F*ck you brain

Migraine

Why?

Why?
a question
I've always asked
when instead of lies
all I wanted was facts

Why?
a question
I've always asked
but you shut me down
shut me up, so then I asked

Again
and again
and again…

Why?
a question
I've always asked
but I had to be silent
wasn't that hard a task

Why?
a question
I've always asked

but instead of lies
you gave me the facts
as you saw them
when I asked
so I masked
all the hurt and the pain

Again
And again
And again…

Why?
a question
I've always asked
when all I would want
was to be heard
wasn't that hard a task

Why?
a question
I've always asked
and didn't get the facts
because the facts were just masked.

Sadness

Sadness
unexplored sadness
hidden sadness
pushed to the depths of my soul sadness
ignored sadness
invisible sadness
silent sadness.

Sits in my chest
sits in my soul
takes root.

I water it with despair
I cultivate it with shame
I prune it with self-loathing

and it grows
it entwines my inner being
like barbed wire viciously wrapped around my
heart.

It continues to engulf my very being and
insidiously hardens my sensitive soul
until it's unrecognisable.

Until that one moment,
on that one day,
when my mind finds the strength to stand up and
say 'enough'
and everything I have been holding onto
deep inside my core
builds
and bursts
and explodes.

Implodes.

The anger
the resentment
the wasted years
the tears
the fears I clung onto, all those years
were never spoken

just shouted
and screamed
all needed to be heard.

In that moment,
my voice returned

and my sadness breathed

I breathed.

I was no longer invisible
I was "mad"…

Me

The day I was given a label
felt like some kind of fable
telling me I'm no longer able

To be ME

The day you walked out of my life
'cause' you said I caused way too much strife
that was it, you wanted a wife

Just not ME

The day I picked myself up
you all said it was just luck
you said I was always too much

I'm just ME

So now I am healing my wounds

all the years of cryin' in my room
listening over and over to tunes

Is it ME?

You all watched me slowly die
not one of you willing to try
to believe me, you said it was lies

It was ME

So again here I am muddling through
always wondering what I should do
So I wrote it all down for you

This is ME

I Wasn't Okay

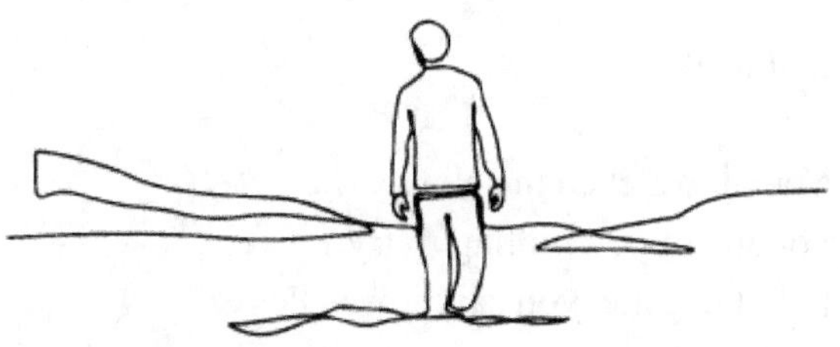

You asked me today
If I was okay
I replied
was dying to confide
you walked away.

You asked me today
If I was okay
I replied
said I hurt inside
you didn't stay.

You asked me today
If I was okay
I replied
said a lie
you talked anyway.

You asked me today
If I was okay

I replied
said I tried
you were miles away.

You asked me today
If I was okay

If I was okay

If I was okay

I replied
said I wanted to die.

You asked me today
If I wasn't okay—why didn't I say?
I replied
said I tried
You walked away.

Being Free

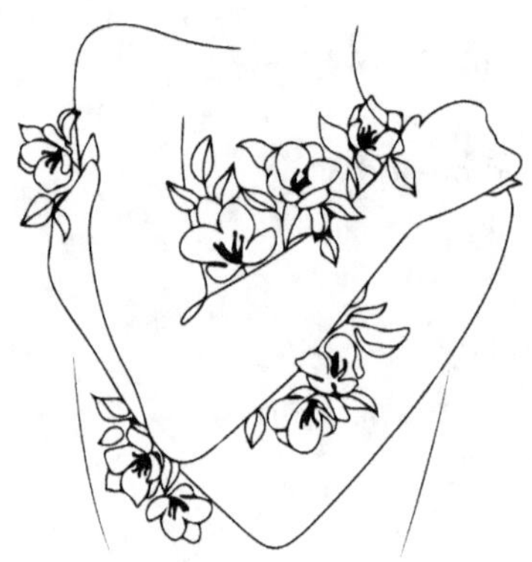

I was told I'd destroyed him
by him himself

I'd cut the ties and the control dissipated
little wonder there was such blind panic

A whole decade had been on hold for me
unhappiness the entire time

Why had he remained for so long
his scant and curt reply;

I felt sorry for you,
I was blind

His pity and charity—I did not need—
it was his

not mine

Being free
is empowering

Being free
allowed me
to reclaim my sanity
Being free
allowed me to address
the stress
that insidiously consumed me

Being free
being free
being free

I am me.

Silence

Silence;
is made of gold
so I'm told
but in this sautéd brain
the slightest drop of the lightest pin
is a din that

I can't escape
I can't erase
I can't gaze out of a window and
block it out
I want to knock it out
gouge it out.

The noise
The noise
The noise

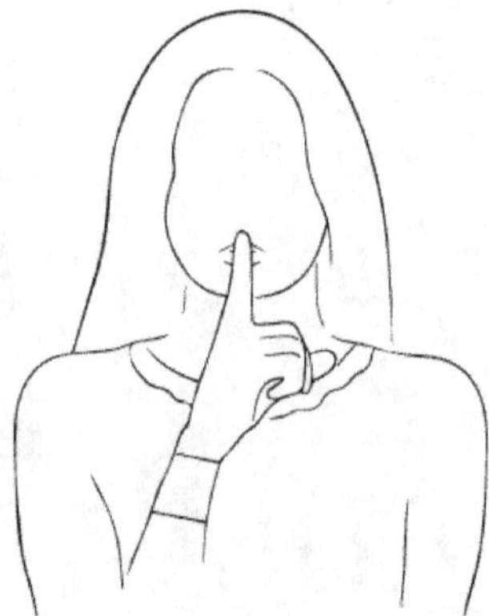

The pain
it's insane
ruins me again
and again
and again

The pain

the noise
but what choice
do I have
but to make the pain
my gain.

My insane
in my brain

Am I insane?

Heard Today

I was heard today
and whilst that's nothing new
I was beginning to wonder
was it really true?

I was heard today
your ears were all mine
you didn't stop or judge me
you gave me all your time.

I was heard today
you listened as I grew
more comfortable with expressing
every pain I'd held onto.

I was heard today
You met me at a level
You didn't shut me down
Or see me as a rebel.

I was heard today
Today I was heard
You listened with such gentleness
To my every word.

I was heard today
It meant the world to me
To finally have someone
To simply see who I can be.

I was heard today,
You helped me feel secure
You said that you'll walk with me
…and didn't close your door.

I was heard today
I was heard today
and you heard all the little things
I didn't even say.

Nature's Wonder

There's a wonder in nature,
when at the sun's rising the silence is slowly yet
purposefully interrupted
by the distant cooing of sleepy wood pigeons
dozing,
before they take flight in search of their early
morning morsel.

The dawn chorus melody,
chirped and twittered, whilst eager starlings
parade the lawn
like elderly gentry pacing a boardroom—hands
behind back—ponderously muttering;
making extraordinary plans for the day.

There's a hierarchy in the apple tree boughs,
several winged visitors making their way
up and down the branches—hopping from one
foot to the other—

waiting patiently for their turn to peck at the suet
laden coconut shells,
dropping the remnants from overloaded beaks
to the pensively waiting sparrows who have yet
to venture so high to retrieve their scrumptious
treats.
A distant feline meowing,
the pitter-patter of border collie dog paws,
constantly sniffing and snaffling,
studiously identifying.

She catches sight of her feathered companions
yet doesn't give chase
—rather seemingly fascinated by their
presence—
slumping down on the patio and instead watches
the lawn; dancing.

There's a wonder in nature,
when at first the morning begins and the
peacefulness seamlessly merges
into birdsong and chatter, breaking the gentle
silence wonderfully and beautifully, for the start
of another glorious day.

My Hope for You

My hope is
whatever struggle you may live with
please know
I understand

My hope for
the days when you cannot convey
your thoughts
your feelings
I understand

My hope for
the darkest of days
in some small way
you can see the light—no matter how slight—
no matter how insignificant it may be
but that it's there offering
some sense of respite

My hope for you
is that you find
just one small positive in your day
even if you have to look
a little longer
a little harder
My hope today
is that you feel gratitude
for the simplest of things
if that was simply waking
and making yourself some hot tea
in your favourite mug
that's okay

My hope for today
is that you acknowledge your journey
you recognise your struggles
and you are able to maintain
a level of emotional wellness
and therapeutic gain

My hope for you today and everyday
is that you are the best you can be
your best is always enough
and I hope in time you'll see

You ARE enough.

You ARE strong.

You ARE worthy.

You ARE loved.

You ARE free.

Goodnight

As we say goodnight
notice the time
notice your breathing
notice the beating of your heart.

Reflect
be mindful
remember the race we are all running is long

You might not be where you want to be right
now—at this very moment;
yet you are not where you were either

If today was a struggle
if today you felt you couldn't endure
rest peacefully now
safe in the knowledge that you did your best.

Focus on your tomorrows—not your yesterdays.

You're a new person
you will continue to refresh and renew
as long as you have the strength to evolve and
the presence of mind to say:
"I can."
Rest easy,
rest well,
and know that wherever you are—it's okay to
just 'be'.

Rain Will Come and Rain Will Go

Rain will come
and rain will go but
we've got to have rain
to make the crops grow
so when you go out
with probably your Dad
just think that rain
isn't really that bad.

Joanne Crane - Aged 9

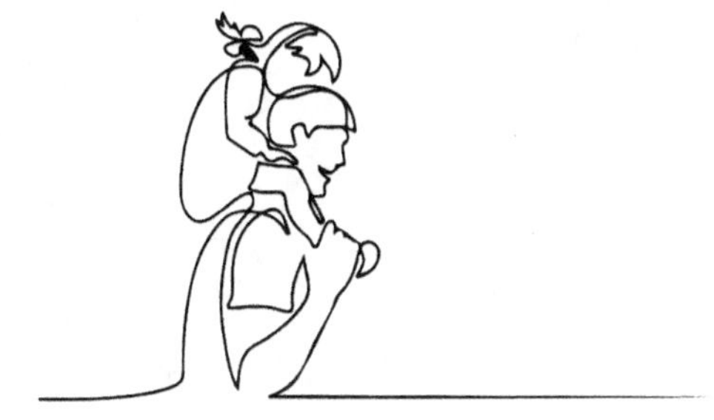

www.ingramcontent.com/pod-product-compliance
Lightning Source LLC
LaVergne TN
LVHW021252200726
843509LV00012B/1648